HOLINESS
unwrapped

ISBN 0-9751555-4-7

Published for The Salvation Army
Australia Eastern Territory by
Commissioner Les Strong.
Produced by The Salvation Army
Communications Department,
Sydney, Australia.
Graphic design and cover concept
by Colleen Danzic.
Cover Photo by Anna Thompson.
Printed in Australia by National
Capital Printing, 22 Pirie Street,
Fyshwick, ACT, 2609.

THE SALVATION ARMY'S
TENTH DOCTRINE

"We believe that it is the privilege of all believers to be wholly sanctified, and that their whole spirit and soul and body may be preserved blameless unto the coming of our Lord Jesus Christ."

(1 Thessalonians 5:23 AV)

TO MAKE US HOLY

> " God's purpose in saving us
> is to create in us the likeness of his Son,
> Jesus Christ, who is the true image of God.
> It is to impart the holiness of Jesus so
> that we may 'participate in the divine nature'
> (2 Peter 1:4). It is to make it possible for us to
> glorify God as Christ's true disciples.
> It is to make us holy. "

(SALVATION STORY, CHAPTER NINE)

To be like Jesus!
This hope possesses me,
In every thought and deed,
This is my aim, my creed;
To be like Jesus,
This hope possesses me,
His Spirit helping me,
Like him I'll be.

— GENERAL JOHN GOWANS

HOLINESS UNWRAPPED

vii

JESUS—
HOLINESS UNWRAPPED

*T*here's no better aim for a Christian than to be like Jesus — and there's no better way to become more like him than to let him live his life in us.

Jesus exemplifies everything we could hope to be and what we ought to be. His goodness shines like a beacon in a world darkened by wrongdoing and self-interest. So it's no surprise that in our complex post-modern era, which often has no clear cut solutions, many Christians find themselves frequently asking the question "What would Jesus do?" Faced with challenging or difficult situations, people the world over look to Jesus for guidance and direction — wanting their actions to reflect him.

Significantly, he left in the gospels guidelines for daily living and lived by them himself. He proved their worth and set us an example. He showed by his own life that what he taught could be successfully embraced. What would be the point of giving us directions if they couldn't be followed? This book won't demand or commend the impossible. That would be counter-productive, because the gap between theory and reality would only bring discouragement.

Instead, the book aims to show that the call to holy living runs throughout Scripture and is both worthwhile and workable. In old testament times, the holy God could seem distant and remote — to be so far above us that he was in "splendid isolation". Then Jesus came. He literally brought God down to earth. And he showed us, in human form, what a holy life was really like. Jesus was holiness unwrapped.

As we see in him what we would like to be, he is more than willing to help us. ✿

PART ONE

To be like Jesus

HOLY

hen we think of Jesus we think of someone who is holy — supremely holy. When we look at ourselves we see imperfections, flaws in our character, disappointments and, if we are honest, we will also admit to being something less than we know we could be. There is a gap that needs bridging.

Jesus came to earth to bridge that gap — and to make it possible for us to live holy lives. He prayed for our holiness (John 17:17-23). In doing so, he indicated it was possible. Would he have prayed for our holiness if it was unattainable?

The word "holy" finds its roots in the Greek New Testament word *hagios* or *hagiasmos*. It speaks of the separateness of God — a strong old testament concept. The almighty, everlasting and all-seeing God was acknowledged as being far above his creation in every sense (Psalm 8). He was uncontaminated, pure, separate — holy (Psalm 96:9).

When Jesus came to live among us as God's Son, he brought his holiness with him. He was God Incarnate — fully human (Philippians 2:7). He was bridging the gap just by being here. More than that, he showed by his own actions what a holy life looked like. He taught how it could be lived. He promised the help we need to live it (John 14:26).

Jesus didn't demonstrate his holiness by wearing a halo round his head, or by keeping a safe distance from people who might contaminate him with their ways or ideas. He demonstrated it by being "tempted in every way, just as we are — yet (being) without sin" (Hebrews 4:15). He remained undefiled, even though he was totally involved in the lives of those around him.

His holiness showed itself in a sinless life, by his purity of motive, by the evidence of grace and truth in all his dealings. He was humble among people, obedient to God the Father, and strong in faith and righteousness.

His holiness showed itself in selfless living, with acts of compassion and mercy, including forgiveness for those who crucified him without cause. He gave full and constant evidence that his love stretches to everyone, and his inner strength was renewed through spending time with the Father.

As we consider these characteristics of Jesus in the pages of this book, we will remind ourselves not only that he calls us to keep our sinful nature under control, but also that he calls us to live positively to his glory among our friends and neighbours (and even our enemies! Matthew 5:44).

Holy living does not come by accident. We need to be intentional about it — to purposefully seek it. We need divine help. Thank God it's there — in Jesus! ◉

6

Reflect on the holiness of God using Psalm 96:1–9 and Isaiah 6:1–8

....
....
....
....
....

Discuss the tension or balance of being separate from the world, yet needing to be active in the world to make an impact for good.

....
....
....
....
....

Describe a holy life.

....
....
....
....
....

Why doesn't holy living come by accident?

....
....
....
....
....

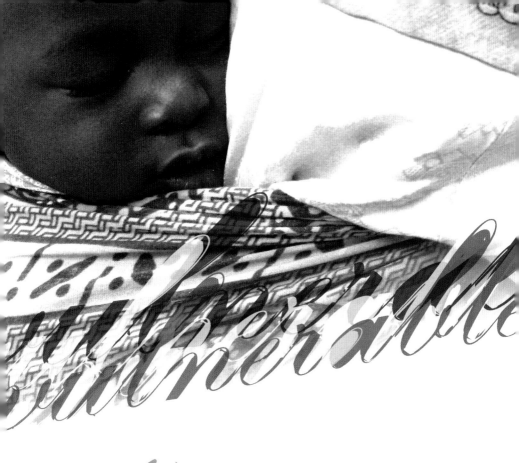

VULNERABLE

To have a newborn baby placed in your arms and to be responsible for looking after this young life can't help but remind any of us of the vulnerability of the baby. He or she is so helpless — totally dependent. Imagine how Mary and Joseph felt when Jesus — the Saviour of the world — was born into their care. Perhaps at Christmas time we catch a glimpse of the wonder of what God was doing, but often the familiarity of the story takes over and we fail to recognise just how vulnerable God was making himself by coming in Jesus to earth.

John's gospel begins by highlighting the irony of the Maker of the heavens coming to earth as a human being and not being recognised (1:10). The One who had ultimate power in the universe made no display of it. Living and growing as we do, he demanded no recognition, but took "the very nature of a servant" (Philippians 2:7).

His vulnerability was evident from the start. Herod tried to have him killed (Matthew 2:16) and Mary and Joseph fled to Egypt to escape the slaughter. When Jesus began his ministry as a man there were others waiting to exploit his vulnerability. His teaching outraged the religious people and the rulers. He refused to be drawn into political power games and spoke God's message — unequivocally, sometimes tenderly, but always truly.

In the end, his vulnerability was laid bare as he was arrested on trumped up charges, falsely accused, wrongly condemned, mocked, beaten, whipped and humiliated. Eventually he was murdered — on a cross. He hung there helplessly — as helpless as a babe it seemed, especially when he cried out "My God, my God, why have you forsaken me?" (Matthew 27:46).

The mystery is that the One hanging on the cross was still God Almighty being true to himself. We — the accusers and murderers — were (and are) the helpless ones. We needed him more than anything else in the world. He alone could save us from ourselves and from our sins.

When scripture tells us that Jesus humbled himself (Philippians 2:8) it only begins to tell the story. Writing to the Romans, Paul recalled that "Even Christ did not please himself" (15:3). He was emphasising the need for endurance and encouragement in the Christian life.

Some of us find it easier than others to be open, to meet people half way, to share what belongs to us. Others find it very difficult. In Christ we see someone who encourages us to dare to make ourselves vulnerable so that we can meet people at their point of need. And he promises his strength to make up for our weakness (2 Corinthians 12:9).

We can remain aloof, strategically distancing ourselves from risk or danger of hurt, or we can make ourselves available to the Christ who has promised to be with us in every situation.

John Wesley said there was no holiness without social holiness. Our quest to be like Jesus will mean we must be ready to live for others as he did. He has promised to be with us (Matthew 28:20). ◉

To consider

In what way does becoming vulnerable assist us in helping others?

....

....

....

....

....

....

....

How helpless are we as people and what can we do about it?
(Romans 5:6 and Philippians 4:13)

....

....

....

....

....

....

To what extent could Jesus be described as having made himself vulnerable?
(Matthew 2:16; Philippians 2:6,7 and Matthew 27:46)

....

....

....

....

....

....

....

....

A PEOPLE PERSON

t's impossible to read the gospels intelligently without realising that Jesus was a people person. There were times when people frustrated him (Mark 8:18) and when he simply had to get away from them (Mark 1:35), but his commitment to people is unquestionable.

Zacchaeus was waiting for someone to believe in him (Luke 19:1–10). He was a disreputable man. Working for the Roman occupiers as a tax collector, he lived by cheating his fellow countrymen. When Jesus stopped to talk to him and invited himself to stay in his home, the transformation in Zacchaeus was remarkable. Zacchaeus believed in Jesus, but Jesus believed in him too — and in what he could become.

Jesus took time to talk to Mary (Luke 10:38–42). He talked to her about the things of God and she drank up every word. Nicodemus, a member of the Jewish ruling council, came to Jesus by night. Jesus shared with him some of his most important teachings (John 3:1–21).

Time and again Jesus took individuals out of the crowd to talk with them and heal them. He spoke to a disreputable woman at a well in Samaria (John 4) and rescued an adulteress from her self-righteous accusers (John 8:1–11).

Even so, people frequently let him down — including those closest to him. The disciples often misunderstood him, made a priority of their own importance and even failed him in the Garden of Gethsemane when he specifically asked them to pray with him at such a crucial time (Matthew 26:36–41). But he coped with their unpredictability and failures — and he also deals with ours today.

Jesus came into the world to make people better — in every good way. He came to build them up, not knock them down. He didn't come to condemn, but to save (John 3:17).

Jesus' followers don't build themselves up to make others look small. They delight in reaching out to others to help them find the hand of Christ. As Paul reminded the Romans (15:2), "Each of us should please his neighbour for his good, to build him up."

We will often be frustrated, disappointed, disillusioned and sometimes wonder why we bother. People make promises they don't keep, take each other for granted and can sometimes be very dislikeable. Jesus never gave up on people — even those who let him down the most. As we try to follow his example, his confidence that others can become better shines through. However other people choose to live or behave towards us, Jesus asks us to still give them the opportunity to find him. ◉

To consider

Why does the ability to be a 'people person' vary from one person to the next?

....
....
....
....
....
....
....
....

What can we learn about Christian living through looking at Jesus' relationships with individuals? (Luke 15:4–7)

....
....
....
....
....
....
....
....

If he gave up on us as readily as we give up on others, where would we be?

....
....
....
....
....
....
....
....

A SERVANT

rom the earliest days of The Salvation Army the two "S"s on the uniform have been interpreted as meaning "Saved to Serve". Salvationists are meant to express their faith — and love for God — in service for others. Service is a hallmark of Salvationism.

The supreme and guiding example of service to mankind comes from Jesus. The concept of God serving his own creation is beyond the comprehension of other religions, but not Christianity. It's at its heart.

Writing to the Philippians, the Apostle Paul drew attention to a standard for disciples of all generations: "Your attitude should be the same as that of Christ Jesus: Who, being in very nature God ...

made himself nothing, taking the very nature of a servant, being made in human likeness" (2:6,7).

Our attitude says a lot about us. A bad attitude can destroy an apparently good action. A good attitude can often make up for lack of achievement. Jesus' attitude was "serving others".

When Jesus announced his own arrival and mission (Luke 4:16–21), he used words from Isaiah 61:1,2 which portrayed him as the Servant of Jehovah: "The Spirit of the Lord is on me, because he has anointed me to preach good news to the poor. He has sent me to proclaim freedom for the prisoners and recovery of sight for the blind, to release the oppressed, to proclaim the year of the Lord's favour".

His ministry was to touch every area of life and he had a strong sense of having been sent. The International Spiritual Life Commission's "call to holiness" reminds us that holy living meets others at their point of need, whatever that may be (see page 109). Like Jesus, we also are "sent to serve".

The realities of life for Jesus — his serving us — included being subjected to the worst of human behaviour. He was betrayed, falsely accused, misjudged, ridiculed, abandoned, whipped, humiliated, nailed to a cross and left to die in pain we can only imagine. For Jesus, servanthood — service to mankind — was not merely running around doing good deeds. It was doing for us what we could not do for ourselves. It was doing what needed to be done. It cost him dearly.

He still serves us, showing the true heart of God. Significantly, his authority seems heightened by his servanthood, not diminished. He is seen to be authentic. When he asks us to serve he is not asking anything he isn't prepared to do himself. The implications for us are clear. If we are to follow Jesus — to become like him — we must embrace servanthood too. In effect, the only authority he gives us is to serve.

Servanthood is not for the proud. It's for the humble (Philippians 2:7). But it doesn't mean constantly giving into other people's opinions or demands. Sometimes it means quite the opposite. A major part of Jesus' servanthood was teaching, giving instruction, correcting and rebuking what was unacceptable to God (Matthew 23:3,13; Mark 9:42; Luke 19:45). He served us by being true to himself. He served by doing what his Father had instructed, by being obedient to his will (Philippians 2:8). So should we.

Jesus' washing of the disciples feet was not only a symbolic act. It expressed the true heart of God (John 13:1–17). "No servant is greater than his master" (v16), he said. If Jesus kneels to serve so should we. ⊛

To consider

What does Jesus' servanthood say about the love of God?

....
....
....
....
....
....

If Jesus' authority was heightened by his servanthood, why are we so reluctant to embrace it?

....
....
....
....
....
....

In what ways is servanthood — service to others — more than simply doing good deeds?

....
....
....
....
....
....

PASSIONATE

quick consideration of instances where Jesus showed passion would probably include the turning over of the tables in the temple where, said Jesus, the money changers had turned God's house into a den of robbers (Luke 19:45). Jesus was obviously incensed at the abuse and misuse of this sacred area and he expressed his anger in no uncertain terms.

He also showed great passion when speaking of the abuse suffered by children at the hands of people who led them into sin. It would be better for such a person, said Jesus, "to have a large millstone hung around his neck and to be drowned in the depths of the sea" (Matthew 18:6). Jesus also had strong words for the Pharisees, with Matthew chapter 23 giving reasons why he saw them as hypocrites.

But Jesus' passion was shown in other ways too. He wept at the sorrow caused by the death of Lazarus (John 11:35). The gospels record him being moved with compassion for individuals with specific needs and for crowds of people. He gave of himself time and time again. He spent his energy and love on them. Most of all, he was so passionate about his people that he died for them. It is not by accident that the last hours of Jesus are known as The Passion and that the true meaning of "passion" is suffering.

We shouldn't assume that passion of itself is a virtue. It can be used to good effect and to bad. Passion gets things achieved, mountains conquered and relief program put in place. It also destroys, distorts and debases. When passion is mentioned in Scripture it is nearly always in the context of being dangerous (e.g. Galatians 5:24; Titus 2:2; 1 Peter 2:11).

General Albert Orsborn, whose holiness songs are referred to a number of times in this book, warned against uncontrolled passion. He wrote:

Come, O Spirit, take control
Where the fires of passion roll;
Let the yearnings of my soul
Centre all in thee.
(The Song Book of The Salvation Army, 630)

The danger is that if we were to act with the same righteous indignation with which Jesus acted, we might easily become hypocrites. Self-righteousness might take over. The kind of passion which leads to fanaticism has been present within religion through the ages. Thousands have been burned at the stake and millions have died in wars in the name of religion — many (incredulously) in the name of Christ.

Passion given free reign wreaks havoc. The passion needed for a holy life is the passion which was in Christ — the passion to do his Father's will whatever the personal cost and however that should be expressed. Put simply, the holy life hands over its passions — all of them — to Jesus, so they can be centred in him, controlled by him, released by him.

General Albert Orsborn has some more words to help us:

Love with passion and with patience,
Love with principle and fire,
Love with heart and mind and utterance,
Serving Christ my one desire.
(The Song Book of The Salvation Army, 522) ✤

To consider

When the Bible speaks of passion it is usually with a warning
(Hosea 7:6,7; Galatians 5:24; Titus 2:12 and 3:3). Why?

....
....
....
....
....
....
....
....
....
....
....
....

In what ways did Jesus use his passion for good?
(Mark 1:41; 6:34 and 8:2; John 3:16)

....
....
....
....
....
....
....
....
....
....
....
....

WITHOUT SIN

e know from human nature that we have a natural inclination to do what we ought not to do. We see children struggling with their behaviour from an early age. We read of Adam and Eve's curiosity and disobedience. We see it in ourselves at every age. The Bible calls these wilful actions "sin" (Romans 3:9,10). Today we usually refer to them as wrongdoing. What we call them doesn't matter so much as being prepared to admit we each have this inclination, and that we need to do something about it.

The Apostle Paul wasn't afraid to face the truth and he bemoaned his own shortcomings. "For what I do is not the good I want to do; no, the evil I do not want to do — this I keep doing" (Romans 7:19). Our behaviour tells us we are not without sin. In contrast, Jesus was without sin

(Hebrews 4:15). He was tempted, but didn't give in to temptation and Scripture records that fact.

When Jesus was baptised in the Jordan river by John the Baptist, it was not to rid himself of sin. It was to demonstrate to the world that he was completely surrendered to his Father's will. It was also part of the process by which he totally identified with the people he came to save — sinners.

The affirmation he received from God the Father was unequivocal: "You are my Son, whom I love; with you I am well pleased" (Luke 3:22).

In this Jesus was acknowledged as holy, set apart for God's will, but his next steps took him to the wilderness — to face temptation. We are told he conquered temptation being "full of the Holy Spirit" (Luke 4:1). Having been tempted he understands our needs from experience and, by the same Holy Spirit, can give us the strength to resist temptation, controlling our sinful tendencies.

Sin weakens us. Our wrongdoing brings us shame. We may not always admit it — or even realise it — but it inevitably makes us less than we ought to be and has a negative effect on our daily living. Ultimately, it's not just a matter of what we might do, but of what we are becoming or have become.

Because Jesus was without sin he could be trusted. His words rang true. He did what he said and lived out what he preached. He was dependable. Added to that, it meant he retained the spiritual power to do his Father's will. Any sin on his part would have undermined his authority. There would have been no victory at Calvary. "It is finished!" would have had a hollow ring to it (John 19:30). But it didn't, it was the triumphant cry of our Redeemer.

When we compromise with evil, we are weakened spiritually. We are not as effective as we could be for God. Paul knew this and asked: "Who will rescue me?" (Romans 7:24). His answer was Jesus (v25). Thankfully, forgiveness is available and renewal can occur.

Paul expresses thanks to Jesus for the grace, strength and power he gives to those who ask (Ephesians 1:17–21). We do not have to sin. We have the means whereby we can choose not to sin and call on Jesus to win the battle.

To consider

If the Apostle Paul had problems with doing wrong what does this say for us? (Romans 7:19)

....

....

....

....

....

....

....

....

What was Paul's way out of the predicament? (Romans 7:24,25)

....

....

....

....

....

....

What encouragement does Romans 8:1,2 give in our quest for holy living?

....

....

....

....

....

....

....

PURE IN HEART

hoosing not to sin and finding strength to avoid wrongdoing, are significant steps to becoming the person God intends us to be. Asking him to purify our heart takes things further. It isn't only about not doing what should be avoided, it is about allowing God to make us what we should be. It is about who we are and what kind of person we are becoming.

Jesus' purity of heart showed itself in his selflessness. His motives were unselfish. He gave himself totally — to us and for us — in every good way, because he knew we needed him.

When he called others to "die to self" (Luke 9:23) and follow him, he already knew from his own self-denying what he was asking others to do.

There is no pure heart in someone whose personal wants and appetites come first. Scheming for our own ends, or manipulating other people (or situations) to our advantage, are in painful contrast to the holy life.

Jesus promised in the beatitudes that the pure in heart would see God (Matthew 5:8). But we cannot manufacture our own pure heart. We aren't capable of it. The cleansing must come from the one who alone can do it. It is a work of grace and it can only take place in humble, repentant people.

So, essentially, Jesus was talking about people whose hearts are made clean by God. This is the Holy Spirit's work. When he is invited into our lives — when our spiritual birth takes place (John 3:3) — the refining fire of the Holy Spirit purifies. We are made new. A fresh start takes place. We are cleansed, made fit to be indwelt by God's Spirit and empowered for living the holy life. A heart cleansed by God involves a washing away of all that has been unholy, and it also indicates motives becoming purified, desires being refined and an intention to live a life surrendered to God.

Leslie Taylor-Hunt described it this way:

Cleanse, thou refining flame
All that is mine;
Self only may remain
If thou refine.
Fix the intention sure,
Make my desire secure,
With love my heart keep pure,
Rooted in thee.
(The Song Book of The Salvation Army, 416)

The words express a movement of self Godwards. They indicate a willingness for "self" to be refined. They demonstrate dependence on God. They don't claim sinless perfection or that God's work on us and in us is finished. Quite the reverse. They are a prayer that the Holy Spirit will keep doing his work — by rooting our intentions and desires in the love of God himself.

Ultimately, a cleansed, renewed heart is an undeserved gift. It comes from a gracious God to those honest and humble enough to want it. A purified heart is an indescribable blessing! ◉

To consider

There is no better human condition than knowing you have been given a clean heart. Discuss.

....
....
....
....
....
....
....
....

How easy is it for our best motives to become tainted with some self–interest?

....
....
....
....
....
....
....

What part does humility play in the making of a pure heart? (Matthew 18:2–4)

....
....
....
....
....
....
....
....

FULL OF GRACE AND TRUTH

eneral John Larsson described Jesus as "The man perfectly filled with the Spirit". His book of that title shows Jesus as the supreme example of the Spirit of God fully indwelling a human being. God was in Christ (2 Corinthians 5:19) — and it showed. No room was given for what was unholy. The will of God was the will of Christ. The power of Christ was the power of God. When John introduces Jesus at the beginning of his gospel he defines him as being "full of grace and truth" (1:4).

Grace and truth go together in Jesus in full measure. They balance each other, complement each other and together show the heart of God. They are the perfect combination.

Truth indicates honesty, openness, nothing hidden. It has always been possible to distort, exaggerate, twist, deny, half-tell, ignore or reject the truth. But in Jesus — who called himself the Truth (John 14:6) — truth is personified. Also introduced by John as the Word (1:1), Jesus speaks transparently to the world without any falsehood. While on earth he represented the Father with supreme authenticity (John 15:15) and the words he spoke had eternal quality. As the Truth, Jesus presented the one and only standard by which we should measure our own living.

The truth is, of course, that not one of us has lived without sin. We have "fallen short" of the glory of God (Romans 3:23) and it shows. The truth condemns us. As we have discovered, it is no use trying to hide the fact, either from ourselves or from God.

This is where grace steps in (Romans 3:24). Titus speaks of Jesus in this way: "For the grace of God that brings salvation has appeared to all men" (2:11).

Grace is perhaps best defined as the undeserved favour of God. It is God seeing our wrongdoing and shortcomings against his standard of truth, and providing the means by which we can be forgiven, restored, renewed — made right with him.

God's grace doesn't run out. We can't use up our quota in one gigantic confession. As long as we live we can turn in repentance, sincerity and need to God and find his grace — and needing God's grace is a lifetime's experience.

If we want to be like Jesus, it's best to embrace the truth he brings, and not avoid what General Albert Orsborn called the Saviour's "kind, but searching eye". It's in embracing the truth about ourselves that we find God's grace and the freedom to be ourselves.

Another of Albert Orsborn's songs marries truth and grace in this way:

I have no claim on grace;
I have no right to plead;
I stand before my maker's face
Condemned in thought and deed.
But since there died a Lamb
Who, guiltless, my guilt bore,
I lay fast hold on Jesus' name,
And sin is mine no more.

(The Song Book of The Salvation Army, 290)

Truth and grace go together in the holy life. ❀

To consider

Consider whether it is possible to receive God's grace without first facing the truth about ourselves?

....
....
....
....
....
....
....
....

How well-balanced are truth and grace in (my) individual life?

....
....
....
....
....
....
....

If we receive God's grace, how readily should we offer it to others?

....
....
....
....
....
....
....
....

A MAN OF PRAYER

esus was a man of prayer. The gospels show that he constantly kept in touch with God the Father by taking time to pray.

He prayed when he was alone (Mark 1:35), withdrawing from the crowd to give prayer his full attention (Luke 5:16). Sometimes he prayed all night (Luke 6:12). He drew strength from his relationship with his Father. He was energised in Spirit from these encounters and his motives were kept holy as he was able to determine his priorities.

He prayed with his disciples (Luke 9:18). He prayed during deeply personal moments — such as his baptism (Luke 3:21) — and he prayed when he was engaged in day-to-day ministry (Luke 10:21). He prayed in his darkest moments — as at Gethsemane (Luke 22:41) and when he was dying (Luke 23:34). Prayer was natural to Jesus. It should be natural to us. It is vital to holy living.

Jesus was asked for guidance in prayer (Luke 11:1) and he gave it. He encouraged everyone to think of God as their loving heavenly Father (Matthew 6:6). People could come to their Father with confidence, knowing he was ready to accept them (Matthew 7:11). God even knows what we need before we ask, he said (Matthew 6:8).

From this reassuring basis, Jesus spoke about what we should pray for and how we should pray. There's no need to babble on or to try to impress God, he said (Matthew 6:6,7). It's a mistake to think we have to attract God's attention, or to imagine that the more we say the more he'll take notice of us.

What we need most of all is to come quietly and humbly before God in open honest relationship. Time set aside to be with God is invaluable, and prayer can take place anywhere at any time.

And the beauty of it is, we don't need to pretend to be different or better than we are. Prayer gives us opportunity to express thanks, say "sorry", as well as to learn from God. It gives opportunity to tell God what is on our heart, and to let God tell us what we need to know and hear.

The specific prayer Jesus taught, which has become known as The Lord's Prayer, gives us a model to live by (Matthew 6:9–13). It highlights respect for God, making his will our priority. It reminds us of the need to forgive others as God has forgiven us and that God, who can keep us from sinning, is ultimately in control of all things. It is not a series of requests for an easy, favoured life, but a prayer that will bring us into deep, fulfilling, holy relationship with him.

Jesus told us to pray for others — even those we find difficult (Matthew 5:44) — to ask God for workers (Matthew 9:38), and to have faith when we pray (Matthew 17:20).

Jesus also prayed for us — for our sanctification, our holiness (John 17:20) — so it was the prayer of God himself that we should be holy. Prayer is not an optional extra in holy living — and God asks us to join him in spirit and intercession as we pray for his world.

> You are with us, interceding
> For a world that is rejecting you again;
> We are with you, and believing
> That our faith and love
> Will move the hearts of men.
> By your Spirit energise us
> And encircle us with light and love and grace;
> Make us worthy to join with you
> Interceding for the human race.
> *(Joy Webb)* ❧

To consider

Why is prayer vital to holy living?

....
....
....
....
....
....
....
....

What lessons can we draw from the prayer life of Jesus?

....
....
....
....
....
....
....
....

What are the most important aspects of prayer taught by Jesus?

....
....
....
....
....
....
....
....

CONSECRATED

here were no half measures with Jesus. He not only came to be with and among us, he also came to give himself for us and to do so completely. He consecrated (sanctified) himself to the will of his Father and never deviated from it.

The old covenant (Testament) had proved impossible to keep. The Law made its demands with The Ten Commandments at the centre, but, as Jesus showed in the Sermon on the Mount, the spirit of the Law was not being kept, let alone the letter of the Law. Something new and better needed to happen. Jesus himself was the answer.

The fact is that Jesus came to do for us what we could not do for ourselves. The old covenant was in tatters because its demands had not been met (Hebrews 8:13). The new covenant, promised in Jeremiah 31:32–33, wouldn't abolish the need for obedience, but by "writing his laws on human hearts", God would give us his presence to help meet the covenant's demands.

It's no exaggeration to say that Jesus wrote the new covenant with his own blood. By doing so, he found his way into our hearts by love which is as unequalled as it is unfathomable. At The Last Supper Jesus gave his disciples an insight into the cost of his love. Taking a cup filled with wine he told them that the cup marked a "new covenant in my blood, which is poured out for you" (Luke 22:20). He also broke bread and, in giving it to them, told them that this was his body "given for you" (22:19). The new covenant was costing him everything. What would be their response? Unbelievably perhaps, their response was to argue about who was the greatest (Luke 22:24). Nevertheless, Jesus remained committed and consecrated to the task. A promise is a promise. A covenant is a covenant. There can be nothing more sacred or binding than a covenant made with and by God.

We make promises every day. Sometimes we make them officially or legally. In the Church we make promises to God at various times and on specific occasions. We make promises in the songs we sing and in the prayers we speak on a regular basis. Sometimes we give them more thought than others and sometimes we dare to make a covenant.

There are those who avoid making promises for fear of failing to keep them. Some make them and later regret it. Others find help from God to keep them.

Today we have the privilege of the presence of the Holy Spirit in our lives. It is he who can empower us. It is he who gives us strength and grace to keep our part of the covenant. When we are aware of our failures, inadequacies and sinful nature, we have the assurance that the blood of Jesus Christ through which the covenant was sealed still brings us the grace of forgiveness and the joy of acceptance.

Jesus consecrated (sanctified) himself that his disciples might be truly sanctified (John 17:19). His prayer was not only for his disciples but also for "those who will believe in me through their message" (17:20).

We have the privilege of responding to such a prayer by asking that God will work his work of grace in us — and consecrate us to his service. ☉

To consider

In what ways does Jesus show us the true meaning of a consecrated life?

....
....
....
....
....
....
....
....

Jesus sealed the covenant with his blood. What do we bring to the covenant?

....
....
....
....
....
....
....
....

How aware are you of the promises you make to God in the course of worship?

....
....
....
....
....
....
....
....

PART TWO

His Spirit helping me

"YOU MUST BE BORN AGAIN"

ot one of us asked to be born. We had no choice or say in the matter. There was no possibility of selecting our parents or family. The time, place and circumstances into which we were born were determined without any help from us!

In this sense we are not born equally. Some are born into riches, loving homes, a Christian environment and security, while others are born into poverty, terror, faithless societies and injustice. There are all kinds of variations on this. The one equalising fact is that everyone born into the world is fully and immediately loved by God. His love is extended to us all (1 John 4:19). The journey through life to discover and fully enjoy that love is different for everyone, and the road is full of choices.

God doesn't force us into relationship with him. If, having had no say in being born, we decide to turn our back on him, we can. God allows us to exercise our free will. It's not what he wants (1 Timothy 2:4), but he sees no virtue in forcing people respond to his love.

On the other hand, the Bible shows that God's love for us is so strong — so total — that he was able to demonstrate it to the fullest possible extent. Speaking of Jesus' sacrificial death on the cross, when he took the full weight of our sin on his shoulders, John 3:16 records, "God so loved the world that he gave his one and only Son, that whoever believes in him shall not perish but have eternal life". The story is not only one of sacrifice, it is also of victory. The resurrection of Jesus, which demonstrated his unequivocal power over death, makes eternal life possible for us all (1 Corinthians 15:57).

We can still turn our backs on such love, of course, either pretending it didn't happen or rejecting it as not having been requested. But the outcome of God's loving intervention through Jesus, is that we do have a choice in regard to being born — there's the chance of a new birth that affects our ongoing and eternal life. Put simply, we are invited to be "born again" (John 3:3).

In the third chapter of John's gospel, Jesus speaks of two births — our natural one and a spiritual one (verses 5 and 6). He tells us that the spiritual birth is essential to enter the Kingdom of Heaven (verse 3). Whether we choose this or not is up to us. How does it happen? Jesus said it was a mystery — difficult to explain (verse 8), but nonetheless totally effective. Phillips Brooks expressed it like this in his carol:

> How silently, how silently
> The wondrous gift is given!
> So God imparts to human hearts
> The blessings of his Heaven.
> No ear may hear his coming;
> But in this world of sin,
> Where meek souls will receive him, still
> The dear Christ enters in.
>
> *(The Song Book of The Salvation Army, 86)*

There is no question of compromise or deals. The Holy Spirit comes in response to our repentance for wrongdoing. He comes to confirm our complete forgiveness and the opportunity of a fresh start. He comes to make a difference. He comes to give us direction, to teach and prompt us, to equip us by his powerful indwelling presence.

The invitation is ours to make. Welcoming him marks the beginning of the holy life. His Spirit helping me . . . ◉

To consider

Why doesn't God force us into relationship with him?

....
....
....
....
....
....
....
....

Why does being born again mark the beginning of the holy life? (John 3:3–6)

....
....
....
....
....
....
....

What difference does being born again make to our lives?

....
....
....
....
....
....
....
....

"YOU ARE GOD'S TEMPLE"

od has many dwelling places. The Bible is full of them and helps put things in perspective.

When God gave Moses The Ten Commandments he did so from heaven: "You have seen for yourself that I have spoken to you from heaven," he said (Exodus 20:22). Heaven, far above mankind and high in glory was where God was expected to dwell. When Jesus taught his disciples to pray, he began with the words: "Our Father, who art in Heaven". God's in his Heaven — wherever that may be.

God was also encountered on the mountain, Mount Horeb being described as the mountain of God in Exodus 3:1. There Moses met God at the burning bush. He took off his shoes because he was on "holy ground". People still meet God on mountains today. They are aware of his presence and still "look to the hills", gaining strength from God as they do so (Psalm 121).

As the Israelites moved among the nations of the Middle East they took God with them by means of the Ark of the Covenant. The golden lid — the Mercy Seat — was known as the meeting place with God (Exodus 25:22). When the Ark was lost in battle, the people felt God had left them too.

Eventually the Israelite nation began to settle and a Temple was built in Jerusalem. The Ark was placed in the Temple. God was now acknowledged as present in his own house. We still speak of "God's house" when we enter a church.

When Jesus was on earth he talked to a Samaritan woman who wanted to know where God should be worshipped (John 4:20). He told her it was the spirit in which worship was given that mattered, not the place. God is everywhere. It was a concept the psalmist had declared hundreds of years earlier (Psalm 139).

Jeremiah had emphasised that when God made a new covenant with his people, his law would be written "on their hearts" (31:33). Incredibly God's dwelling place would be within human kind. Jesus confirmed this in many ways, especially when he spoke of our being "born again" — inwardly, by his Spirit. He also spoke of his coming again to be in us (John 14:16–19).

God's indwelling was a concept the Apostle Paul highlighted when the Corinthian Church was beginning to become "worldly". "Don't you know you yourselves are God's temple and that God's Spirit lives in you?" he challenged (1 Corinthians 3:16). If we are to be God's temple we must be willing to let him make and keep our hearts fit for his presence. Colonel Brindley Boon wrote this prayer as a song for his own commissioning as an officer:

> I would be thy holy temple,
> Sacred and indwelt by thee;
> Naught then could stain my commission,
> 'Tis thy divine charge to me.
>
> Take thou my life, Lord,
> In deep submission I pray,
> My all to thee dedicating,
> Accept my offering today.
> (The Song Book of The Salvation Army, 786)

Of all the places God lives, our humble human heart is the most precious to him (Psalm 51:10–12); his temple. ⊛

To consider

How are we made fit temples for the Holy Spirit?

....
....
....
....
....
....
....
....

In what ways does our behaviour change when God dwells within us?

....
....
....
....
....
....
....
....

What is the "deep submission" that the song mentions?

....
....
....
....
....
....
....
....

"CHRIST IN YOU"

hen someone is born again of the Holy Spirit, that person enters into a new relationship with God. A new life has begun — a holy life.

It's not something we should take for granted, or be careless about; if so, it will break down (1 Corinthians 3:17). It's a closeness Jesus wanted for his disciples — he prayed for it and he told them so. On the eve of his crucifixion he spoke of a time that was soon coming: "On that day you will realise that I am in the Father, and you are in me, and I am in you" (John 14:20). Such closeness is beyond our understanding, but "Christ in us" confirms God's intention to make it a reality.

When Jesus' forthcoming birth was announced to Joseph in a dream (Matthew 1:23), Joseph was told that the baby would be called "Immanuel", meaning "God with us". This blend of divinity with humanity has been described as the incarnation. When Christ is welcomed into our lives this, too, is described as being incarnational. God himself lives and works out his purposes within humans.

This closeness or union means that for the person who is "born again", God is always present within. He isn't "received" again during different ceremonies or rituals, because he is already there — in the hearts of his people.

His grace is freely and readily accessible. We can speak with him and he with us directly. Although a priest or Christian colleague can help us in our relationship with God, each of us may have our own "personal relationship" with Jesus.

The Salvation Army has preached and developed the concept of personal relationship with Jesus, since its inception. It is uncluttered, uncomplicated, simple — I invite Christ to be Lord of my life, he comes, he lives his life in me, and he confirms his presence in me by the way I am enabled to live (Galatians 2:20).

Although it is clear and simple in its expression, the relationship depends greatly on the grace of God and our willingness to receive it.

General Albert Orsborn described the relationship in sacred terms:

My life must be Christ's broken bread,
My love his outpoured wine,
A cup o'erfilled, a table spread
Beneath his name and sign,
That other souls, refreshed and fed,
May share his life through mine.

Such words, when meant, make our very lives a sacrament. This is incarnational ministry. It is "down-to-earth" with Heaven in charge — the divine and the human working together to do God's will. It requires costly dedication to God.

My all is in the Master's hands
For him to bless and break;
Beyond the brook his winepress stands
And thence my way I take,
Resolved the whole of love's demands
To give for his dear sake.

(The Song Book of The Salvation Army, 512)

The Apostle Paul described this as "Christ in you, the hope of glory" (Colossians 1:27). It is holiness. ☼

To consider

How personal is a "personal relationship" with Jesus?

....
....
....
....
....
....
....
....

What are the implications of God's grace being freely and readily accessible?

....
....
....
....
....
....
....

Discuss the implications for your life of Albert Orsborn's song,
"My life must be Christ's broken bread".

....
....
....
....
....
....
....
....

THE GIFTS OF THE SPIRIT

*I*t is important to realise that any gift that comes from the Holy Spirit is given to the Church rather than merely to an individual. Gifts are given to be used for the purposes of God, and God's good purposes involve everyone.

General Jarl Wahlstrom emphasised this when he stated firmly and clearly: "The gifts of the Spirit are not meant to be worn on the chest like a row of medals. They are given for use in the Church for the benefit of the people."

It is undeniable that the Church has suffered badly from arguments about these gifts. It is also deeply disappointing. The Apostle Paul tried to address the problem in the Early Church where, already, it was sidetracking new Christians from their main purpose.

To the Corinthians he wrote: "There are different kinds of gifts, but the same Spirit" (1 Corinthians 12:4), before pointing out that "to each one the manifestation of the Spirit is given for the common good" (verse 7). He wanted Christians to get things in context (of the Church) and perspective (to use for the common good).

It is significant that when the activity of the Holy Spirit is recorded by Paul in his New Testament letters, more than two thirds of the references are corporate. The Spirit is seen as God's gift to the Church. The Holy Spirit is the great Unifier. We find our identity in him. We belong to each other — and to God — through him. We cannot divorce ourselves from the Body (Romans 12:4,5).

Jesus told his disciples that the proof of their belonging to him was found in their acceptance of each other: "Love one another . . . By this all men will know that you are my disciples, if you love one another" (John 13:34,35).

In his notes on The Foundation and Nature of the Christian Life, Major Cecil Waters points out, "We are not individuals sharing the grace of God in splendid isolation, but individuals caught up in and contributing to a community as a single organism".

In spite of frequent dissention seen in the Church because of controversy, the gifts of the Spirit have a vital role to play. They are "the work of one and the same Spirit," says Paul, pointing out that God "gives them to each one, just as he determines" (1 Corinthians 12:11).

Today many churches and fellowships take time to help their members identify the gifts they have been given by God. They then set about helping them find opportunities for service using those gifts. This is good stewardship, built on the initiative of God, the giver. Some gifts of the Spirit are recorded in 1 Corinthians 12, as well as elsewhere in the New Testament. They demonstrate that God is active in equipping his people in their understanding of his will and in their service for him.

As we embrace the gifts God has given us thus far, we should remain open to his ongoing leadings, being ready to serve in ways which are helpful even though they may not be "our gift". To the Romans Paul wrote: "We have different gifts, according to the grace given us" (12:6). With this reminder Paul emphasised again that all gifts come through divine grace — and this applies to everything we receive from the bountiful, generous hand of God! ◉

To consider

Describe the Body of Christ.

....
....
....
....
....
....
....
....

Although the Holy Spirit is the agent who unites God's people, spiritual gifts have caused much dissention in the Church. Why?

....
....
....
....
....
....
....

If God gives me gifts, what are they for?

....
....
....
....
....
....
....
....

"YOU WILL RECEIVE POWER"

ne of the best qualifications for Christian ministry is a sense of inadequacy — possibly coupled with a sense of unworthiness. Those who think they are clever enough or good enough will have problems — and they will create problems for others. God's work can only be done effectively if we rely on him for our resources.

Shortly before his ascension, Jesus told the apostles: "Do not leave Jerusalem, but wait for the gift my Father promised, which you have heard me speak about. For John baptised with water, but in a few days you will be baptised with the Holy Spirit" (Acts 1:4,5).

The eventual coming of the Holy Spirit into their lives on the Day of Pentecost was a momentous occasion. He was welcomed and received — effecting a dramatic unity among them (Acts 2:1). The great Unifier was doing his work (Acts 2: 42–47).

They had been told to wait, but it wasn't to be a passive waiting — such as just passing the time until something happened. It was to be an active waiting — in essence, a waiting on God. They were to spend time in prayer, seeking the blessing of God. They were to spend time together, ensuring they were united in faith and love. Only when they knew in their hearts that they were ready to receive God, would the Holy Spirit come.

The dramatic coming of the Holy Spirit to the Church began a new chapter. The birth of the Church cannot be repeated, but God still comes to his people, and he still comes only to those who want him to come, to those who pray for his promised presence. It is as necessary today as it was then to wait expectantly and obediently if we are to welcome him into our lives.

The promise also indicated that "power" would be received with the Holy Spirit's coming (Acts 1:8). It wasn't power to use for our own ends, or to pander to our own interests, but power to do God's work. In the same way that Jesus had earlier promised that his Father would give "good gifts" to those who asked him (Matthew 7:11), so this gift of power would come as a resource for mission and ministry.

The Apostle Paul, writing to the Philippians about his varied and demanding experiences as a Christian, concluded: "I can do all everything through him who gives me strength" (4:13).

In the beatitudes Jesus indicated that only those who "hunger and thirst after righteousness" would be filled (Matthew 5:6). He commended those who "know their need of God" (verse 3 NEB) and these are the ones he equips for service today — not necessarily in dramatic ways, but in ways which will see God's Kingdom grow on earth.

William Booth used the coming of the Holy Spirit at Pentecost as the basis for his song, *Send the fire*. The third verse speaks in the direct language of his day of the purpose for which God's power is required:

For strength to ever do the right,
For grace to conquer in the fight,
For power to walk the world in white,
Send the fire!

(The Song Book of The Salvation Army, 203)

The strength and power to live the holy life come only from God. His Spirit helping me . . . ●

64

To consider

Why are senses of inadequacy and unworthiness good characteristics
for a Christian? (Luke 5:8)

....
....
....
....
....
....
....
....

For what reasons does God give us his power? (Acts 1:8)

....
....
....
....
....
....
....

What is his power like? How does it manifest itself?

....
....
....
....
....
....
....
....

PART THREE

Like him I'll be

THE FRUIT OF THE SPIRIT

Measuring or quantifying spiritual experience can't be done. There is no way we can give ourselves marks out of 100 for our behaviour or obedience to God's word and will. Trying to do so would be as foolish as it would be futile.

After all, none of us started our Christian journey from the same place. Some of us were taught the faith from an early age and saw it exampled in our parents. Others were taught the faith well, but had poor examples. Others heard a few snatches of the Gospel to a helpful or less helpful extent, and far too many have been taught to treat the whole "God subject" with suspicion. Put varied intellectual capacity, social interaction, health, tragedy, self-worth and other factors into the equation, and we can see that trying to assess each other's goodness or holy living is inappropriate too.

But we do have a reliable personal check list. The fruit of the Spirit, as listed by Paul in Galatians 5:22, are the Christlike qualities that should be developing — growing — within us. He identifies the fruit as love, joy, peace, patience, kindness, goodness, faithfulness, gentleness and self-control. This is probably not an exhaustive list, but there's no doubt that if we have invited the Holy Spirit into our lives, and he is living his life in us, the evidence of his presence should increasingly be apparent.

The analogy of fruit growing is significant, because it implies moving towards perfection or full maturity. Paul, who both preached and embraced holiness, openly indicated that God was still working on him. He hadn't "arrived" or "been made perfect" (Philippians 3:12). He was moving heavenwards by God's grace (verse 14).

Although we have different personalities and gifts, there is no escaping the fact that if the fruit of the Spirit is not evidenced in us — not seen growing in us — something is wrong and needs attention. These nine clear characteristics of God the Holy Spirit were found in Jesus and by his Spirit they can grow within us. We may develop some more easily than others, but it's not for us to "pick and choose" the ones we like best.

Jesus, through his Spirit, helps us deal with the difficult ones and if we can trust him to do so we will have the joy of identifying how God himself — in a very personal way — is impacting on our daily living. Trust him to do it. ☉

To consider

How would you describe the list of the fruit of the Spirit as recorded in Galatians 5:22? Is there a common thread?

....
....
....
....
....
....
....

Think through the implications on our daily living of having the fruit growing within us.

....
....
....
....
....
....
....

Which fruit do you think needs the most attention in your own life?

....
....
....
....
....
....
....
....

THE FRUIT OF THE SPIRIT IS
LOVE

esus had a lot to say about love. He said that "to love" was the greatest commandment. John says that God *is* love (1 John 4:8). If we are aiming to be like Jesus, love will be at the centre of who we are and what we do.

There are different definitions of the word "love" with a variety of interpretations and usages in Scripture — friendship, sexual love, family love and God's love for his people, to name some. The significance of the word "love" listed among the fruit of the Spirit, is that this is love born of God which can find expression through us.

John has no difficulty making the link. "Dear friends, let us love one another, for love comes from God," he writes (1 John 4:7). He then uses the love of God as shown in Jesus as our supreme example. "This is how God showed his love among us: He sent his one and only

Son into the world that we might live through him. This is love, not that we loved God, but that he loved us and sent his Son as an atoning sacrifice for our sins" (verse 9).

He then says we should follow this example: "Since God so loved us, we also ought to love one another" (verse 11).

John highlights the totality of the love of God — Jesus sacrificing his life for us — to demonstrate the quality of love required from us. We may not be called upon to endure a painful crucifixion, but we are to show love through selfless living and a genuine spirit of giving.

How can we do it? John puts it simply. "If we love one another, God lives in us and his love is made complete in us" (verse 12). It is the indwelling presence of God's Holy Spirit that resources us.

Jesus told his disciples not to pick and choose who they would love. "Love your enemies," he instructed (Matthew 5:44). *The Message* paraphrases what Jesus said next with candid clarity: "If all you do is love the lovable, do you expect a bonus? Anybody can do that" (verse 46).

The essential place of love in the Christian life is perhaps most noticeably emphasised by Paul in his First letter to the Corinthians. He speaks of the gift of prophecy, of faith that can move mountains, of fathoming mysteries and even making the ultimate sacrifice. But "without love, I am nothing", he says (v2), and "I gain nothing" (v3).

If ever we are tempted to think that possessing gifts from God is good enough, Paul urges us to think again. It is the fruit growing in us — especially identified through love — that is the real evidence (1 Corinthians 12:30), "the most excellent way".

Remembering that God's Spirit is most fully expressed through his Body, the Church, the words of Jesus to his disciples shortly before his death are crystal clear. "A new command I give you: Love one another. As I have loved you, so you must love one another. By this will men know that you are my disciples, if you love one another" (John 13:34,35).

Love is the best evidence that we are becoming like Jesus. ⊛

Why is love so essential to Christianity?

....
....
....
....
....

Explore what John means when he says God is Love (1 John 4:8).

....
....
....
....
....

How good are we Christians at loving one another? (John 13:34,35)

....
....
....
....
....

What are the implications of failure to do so?

....
....
....
....
....
....

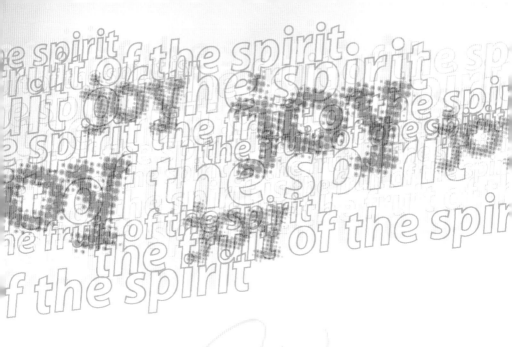

THE FRUIT OF THE SPIRIT IS
JOY

e live in an age where cynicism is part of everyday life. Suspicion and mistrust are not hard to find and it can sometimes be difficult to detect real joy — joy that goes deep in a person.

Joy is among God's gifts to his people. It is a recurring theme through Scripture. In Galatians 5:22 it is listed among the fruit of the Spirit.

There can be various reasons for not feeling joyful. Tragedy, loss, disappointment and betrayal don't produce joyful feelings. This is natural, and a forced kind of joy is no joy at all. Such instances are not the issue, though the indwelling of the Holy Spirit certainly brings comfort and strength at such times.

Psalm 16 makes the bold declaration to God that "In your presence is fullness of joy" (verse 11, RAV). It follows then, that if we are indwelt by the Holy Spirit, if he lives within us, his presence will ensure our deep joy — "fullness of joy". The experience speaks of relationship with God, of companionship and trust that brings richness of security. It brings knowledge that we are loved, cared for and valued to the last degree. It brings joy.

This is in harmony with the shorter catechism which says that "enjoying God forever" is one of the reasons for which we were created. If we don't experience this joy something is missing — something we were intended to have.

In the New Testament joy and gladness are specifically and frequently related to the whole life of the Church. Joy is not something we were intended to experience in isolation. In the same way that Paul encourages us to "weep with those who weep", he expects us to "rejoice with those who rejoice" (Romans 12:15). We are meant to feel each other's sorrows and joys because we belong to one another. We are united by and in the Holy Spirit who dwells in us.

When the early day Salvationists sang "Joy! joy! joy! There is joy in The Salvation Army" *(The Salvation Army Song Book 807)*, they may well have been more theologically correct than they knew. Joy should be a natural part of our corporate worship, and sharing the joy of the Lord should be the witness and experience of the Church. Without it we insult or neglect the gift of salvation we have undeservedly received.

Joy is not merely a consequence of faith. It is an integral part of our total relationship with God. It is also linked with the promise of what is to come.

Isaiah 12:3 speaks of drawing water from the wells of salvation — with joy. It is our salvation that fires our joy. It is the anticipation of eternity which confirms the lasting nature of our joy.

Joy speaks of Christian maturity. To hide or suppress it can demonstrate the reverse.

Just before Jesus left the disciples he is recorded as praying to his Father, "I am coming to you now, but I say these things while I am still in the world, so that they may have the full measure of my joy within them" (John 17:13).

The full measure of the joy of Christ? It should be growing within us all the time.

To consider

Compare cynicism and joy and their place within Christian fellowship.

....
....
....
....
....
....
....
....

What brings the "full measure of the joy of Christ"? (John 17:13)

....
....
....
....
....
....
....

What prevents us from experiencing or sharing our joy?

....
....
....
....
....
....
....
....
....

THE FRUIT OF THE SPIRIT IS
PEACE

                              he peace which comes from God defies description. Philippians 4:7 says it "transcends all understanding". It has to be experienced to be believed.

When people are asked what they would ask for if they could be granted one wish, near the top of the list is "world peace". We want a world without discord, without hatred, without war. This kind of peace is hoped and prayed for frequently in the Old Testament (Psalm 122:6). The Israelites had their battles with other nations — and they had their constant spiritual battles with God and his laws. Their sin repeatedly kept them estranged from their God and Jeremiah's words highlighted their plight: "We hoped for peace but no good has come, for a time of healing but there was only terror" (8:15). Peace comes at a price. It has to be worked for, achieved, cultivated and maintained. It doesn't occur automatically.

The peace which Jesus gives is a gift. It is undeserved and cannot be earned. But it will not occur automatically. It comes to those who give God his rightful place in their lives.

The Hebrew word for peace, *shalom*, goes further than the "absence of war" definition. It speaks of well-being and totality, and the adjective *shalem* indicates wholeness. Wholeness and holiness go together. Today we speak of a holistic approach to life. In the Christian life what we are in fact seeking is that God makes us whole. He forgives, heals and restores us. Then he indwells us, fills us with himself. We are at harmony with him, at one, at peace.

The barriers to such peace come from our own wilfulness. Discord arises when we insist on going our own way, or rejecting to do what we know God is asking us to do. We may even get to the point where we no longer hear God because we have turned a deaf ear to him once too often.

As we have noted, Jesus spoke of love and joy to his disciples on the eve of his crucifixion. He wanted them to understand their importance. He also spoke about peace as his lasting gift. "Peace I leave with you; My peace I give to you. I do not give to you as the world gives" (John 14:27). It was a peace that would calm their troubled hearts.

This peace didn't mean the absence of conflict or hardship — and it is important for us to realise this. It was an inner peace that would always be there whatever happened. "I have told you these things," said Jesus, "so that in me you may have peace. In this world you will have trouble. But take heart! I have overcome the world" (John 16:33).

The New Testament emphasises the corporate blessing of peace upon God's people. "Therefore, since we have been justified through faith, we have peace with God through our Lord Jesus Christ" (Romans 5:1). Alongside this is the call to God's people. "Let the peace of Christ rule in your hearts, since as members of one body you were called to peace" (Colossians 3:15).

There will be no peace in the heart of the believer — or at the heart of a fellowship — if Christ doesn't rule. But with Jesus as Lord of our life the peace which transcends all understanding will guard our hearts and our minds into eternity (Philippians 4:7). ◉

To consider

Try to describe the indescribable — 'the peace of God, which transcends all understanding' (Philippians 4:7).

....
....
....
....
....
....
....

Discuss the difference between the peace which is 'absence of war' and 'peace of heart'.

....
....
....
....
....
....
....

How does peace rule in our hearts? (Colossians 3:15)

....
....
....
....
....
....
....
....

THE FRUIT OF THE SPIRIT IS
PATIENCE

his is the age of "instant" everything. What once we had to wait hours, days, weeks or even years for, we can now access in a moment. We have come to expect speedy resolutions to our problems, quick answers to our queries and, if there appear to be unnecessary hold-ups, we soon want to know why.

But still there is the need for patience – and, without knowing how to use it, we act like spoiled children, unable to wait for Santa Claus.

In Scripture, patience is linked to long-suffering and perseverance. Because patience is a fruit of the Spirit of God, it reminds us, first of all, that God is patient. He is long-suffering – particularly over our waywardness and sins.

When God made covenant with Moses he emphasised then his patience with us, his creation; "The Lord, the Lord, the compassionate and gracious God, slow to anger, abounding in love and faithfulness, maintaining love to thousands, and forgiving wickedness . . ." (Exodus 34:6).

When Christians of the early Church were growing tired of waiting for the Lord's return Peter reminded them that "with the Lord a day is like a thousand years, and a thousand years are like a day" (2 Peter 3:8). Then he reminded them of a positive reason for the Lord's patience. "The Lord is not slow in keeping his promise, as some of you understand slowness. He is patient with you, not wanting anyone to perish, but everyone to come to repentance" (v9). We have good cause to thank God for his patience with us.

If patience is a characteristic of God, it follows that it is a fruit of his Spirit and should show itself in the way we relate to other people – especially those who "try our patience". It is not enough to shrug our shoulders and confess to "not suffering fools gladly". We are to allow God to work his work of patience in us.

Paul had more than his "fair share" of difficult Christians. He urged Timothy, "Correct, rebuke and encourage – with great patience and careful instruction" (2 Timothy 4:2). The word of God encourages us to do the same as we pursue the holy life.

There is also another area needing attention. It is the impatience which wants God to sort everything (and perhaps everyone) out now. If he is God, why doesn't he do something about all the wrongs and injustices – now? Must we wait until the end of time for his love and justice to show themselves fully and ultimately together? This is the patience of endurance.

The writer to the Hebrews has some words for us. "Let us throw off everything that hinders and the sin that so easily entangles, and let us run with perseverance the race marked out for us. Let us fix our eyes on Jesus, the author and perfector of our faith . . ." (12:1,2).

Jesus is at the beginning and the end of our walk of faith. This walk of faith requires trust – trust that what God has promised he will supply. Impatience with God signifies a lack of trust in him. As we allow him to live his life in us, so his patience, his long-suffering, his perseverance will grow within us too. ❀

To consider

How patient is God with us?

....
....
....
....
....
....
....
....

Psalm 37:7 encourages us to wait patiently for the Lord. Why?

....
....
....
....
....
....
....

To what extent might my lack of patience indicate a lack of trust in God?

....
....
....
....
....
....
....
....

THE FRUIT OF THE SPIRIT IS
KINDNESS

indness is
a quality that everyone would expect Christians to
possess. Unkind Christians are a contradiction in terms
— and, where they apparently exist, they will be doing
untold damage to the Christian cause.

Kindness is also a quality that everybody is expected
to have, whether Christian or not. It is seen as part of
what any decent person should be. Shakespeare wrote of
the "milk of human kindness" and spoke of being "cruel
to be kind". It is part and parcel of everyday life.

If we look at kindness as a fruit of the Spirit, we
acknowledge that the kindness to which Galatians
5:22 refers comes from God. Throughout Scripture
God's kindness is praised by his unworthy creation. It
is expressed in inexhaustible ways and many of them
are highlighted in Psalm 103 which thanks God for

crowning us with "loving-kindness and tender mercies" (v4 RAV).

Kindness is pro-active. We initiate acts of kindness. If we don't initiate them they probably don't happen. But they will happen from hearts that are filled with God. He prompts and reminds us of what needs to be done, and what attitudes need to be shown.

In the Sermon on the Mount Jesus teaches that we should take the initiative. "Do good to those who hate you," he says (Matthew 5:44). In the same sermon he wraps things up like this: "So in everything, do to others what you would have them do to you, for this sums up the Law and the Prophets" (7:12). The teaching couldn't be clearer.

The New Testament demonstrates that Christians should be "clothed in" and express kindness as a natural outcome of their holy life in Christ. Colossians 3:12 says: "Therefore, as God's chosen people, holy and beloved, clothe yourselves with compassion, kindness, humility, gentleness and patience". All these qualities come from God, so they should be expressed in Christian living.

When Paul was commending his ministry to the Corinthians he listed kindness among the evidences (2 Corinthians 6:6), and Peter lists it too among the qualities that Christians should have (1 Peter 1:7).

Paul's masterful passage on love, includes this: "Love is patient, love is kind," but he immediately followed this with: "It does not envy, it does not boast, it is not proud" (1 Corinthians 13:4). These issues have to be dealt with too if we are not to be unkind.

But all this teaching is based on God's overwhelming kindness to us. In his letter to the Ephesians Paul is overwhelmed by "the incomparable riches of (God's) grace, expressed in his kindness to us in Christ Jesus" (2:7). The same theme comes through in the letter to Titus. "But when the kindness and love of God our Saviour appeared, he saved us, not because of righteous things we had done, but because of his mercy" (3:4).

If God has shown such kindness to us, we must express the same quality of kindness to others. Kindness should be a natural expression of our life in Christ — the Christ from whom we have already received more kindness than we could ever deserve.

To consider

Consider how often Scripture speaks of the loving kindness of God.

....
....
....
....
....
....
....
....

Is kindness something we usually need to initiate? If so, could we be neglecting to develop this fruit?

....
....
....
....
....
....
....

Can there be such a thing as an unkind Christian?

....
....
....
....
....
....
....
....

THE FRUIT OF THE SPIRIT IS GOODNESS

ost of us know someone — probably more than one person — who just seems to be filled with goodness. Everything about them seems wholesome, kind and loving. They somehow make us feel better for having met them and they give us faith in human nature. Sometimes we complain that there don't seem to be so many of these people around as when we were younger. Perhaps it has always been the same!

One of their most endearing qualities is that they apparently don't realise that we think of them in this way. Perhaps that's because goodness has a close association with humility. In these people we believe we are witnessing a holy life — someone living close to God, his Spirit helping them.

In Scripture the word "good" can be applied to "good food" as well as to the "Good Shepherd". But true goodness is seen as coming only from God. As with holiness, there is no goodness apart from him. So when a rich young man came to Jesus asking what was good, Jesus put things in perspective. 'Why do you ask me about what is good?' he asked. "There is only One who is good" (Matthew 19:17).

It is in this spirit that Harriette Auber wrote:

And every virtue we possess,
And every victory won,
And every thought of holiness,
Are his alone.

(The Song Book of The Salvation Army , 200)

The Psalmist was bold in his affirmation and his call: "Taste and see that the Lord is good" (Psalm 34:8). Goodness comes from God and those whose lives it touches, can't help but feel the benefit of it.

But even the strongest saints haven't always found things easy. Paul confessed: "For what I do is not the good I want to do; no, the evil I do not want to do — this I keep on doing" (Romans 7:19). The path of holiness is a lifelong journey.

So Paul follows with this advice for the Romans: "Do not conform any longer to the pattern of this world, but be transformed by the renewing of your mind (12:2). He continues: 'Then you will be able to test and approve what God's will is — his good, pleasing and perfect will."

Goodness is also synonymous with what is right. When the Law was given, the Israelites were urged to "do what is right and good in the Lord's sight" (Deuteronomy 6:18). When faced with tough choices goodness will choose what is right.

In closing his first letter to the Thessalonians, Paul emphasised again the uncompromising fight that goodness has with evil. "Hold on to the good," he says. "Avoid every kind of evil" (5:21,22). It reiterates the uncompromising challenge of his words to the Romans: "Do not repay anyone evil for evil" (12:17).

Goodness doesn't delight in retaliation, in other people's misfortunes or downfall. To do this damages our relationship with God. It undermines all he is trying to do in and through us. So Paul concludes with "Do not be overcome by evil, but overcome evil with good" (verse 21).

Be good! ⚙

To consider

How much of what I do is simply for goodness' sake?

....
....
....
....
....
....
....
....

If goodness comes alone from God what does that say about my life of holiness (Matthew 19:17)?

....
....
....
....
....
....
....

By what means do we overcome evil with good (Romans 12:21)?

....
....
....
....
....
....
....
....

THE FRUIT OF THE SPIRIT IS FAITHFULNESS

hink of yourself as unfaithful. Imagine you frequently fail to keep your word. You tell lies, cover them up with fanciful stories and do things in secret which damage your friend's reputation. You have forgotten why other people are loyal and trustworthy, and everything you do is for your own ends. You are simply using other people as it suits you.

It isn't a good picture — and it spells out why faithfulness is an essential part of our Christian walk. The gospels show Jesus as being completely dependable and true to his word. They tell us that he is the Truth (John 14:6). If we aim to "be like Jesus" we cannot avoid faithfulness. It is integral to who we are and what we do.

The word "faith" implies belief in something. Belief in Jesus Christ speaks of our trust in him, arising out of personal conviction. If we are faithful to him we live by what we believe he requires from us. If we have made promises to him, we live by those promises. We honour his promises to us by honouring our promises to him. The issue is straightforward.

But there is something in the human condition that disappoints and, it seems, defies even the best intentions. There is a rebellious streak in us, a resistance to the control of promises made or to the obligations of our social life — and unfaithfulness rears its ugly head. Usually it is those who trust us the most who are most likely to be hurt. We need to think seriously and deeply before acting unwisely. History is littered with "if onlys".

The Old Testament has its own record of unfaithfulness. In particular, Israel, who received from God all that was good and who was deeply loved, is frequently depicted as being unfaithful and ungrateful. Her unfaithfulness grieved God deeply (Jeremiah 9:1–6). This passage, in particular, shows the havoc that unfaithfulness causes in community, among friends and with God. Jeremiah also speaks of the Israelites as being "faithless" (3:6). Their lack of faith in God was the cause of wayward behaviour.

Significantly, the New Testament tells us that faith is a gift from God. "For it is by grace you have been saved, through faith — and this not from yourselves, it is the gift of God" (Ephesians 2:8), says Paul. The faith we have been given, gives hope that exceeds all other hopes (Hebrews 11:1). It plants in us a steadfastness and deep trust in the eternal God himself, from whom all resources flow and from whom all empowering to live the good life comes.

Faith is not sight. We do not have complete knowledge of God or the future. Heaven's mysteries are not ours to see. We are given faith — faith to live by, faith to develop, faith that will strengthen every time we truly exercise it. We are given faith that is alive, that challenges us, encourages us, supports us and ultimately grows within us, giving evidence that it is indeed a fruit of the Spirit.

As we look to Jesus as the source of our faith, Scripture affirms his faithfulness time after time. Writing to the Corinthians, Paul testifies that "God, who has called you into fellowship with his Son Jesus Christ our Lord, is faithful (1.1:9). Of God's promise to sanctify his people "through and through", he writes, "The one who calls you is faithful. He will do it" (1 Thessalonians 5:24). Trust him. ☉

To consider

Faithfulness to God is shown in our faithfulness to others. Discuss.

....
....
....
....
....
....
....

Scripture tells us God is faithful to sanctify his people "through and through"
(1 Thessalonians 5:23,24). Are we trusting him to do that?

....
....
....
....
....
....
....

What would life be like if God was unfaithful?

....
....
....
....
....
....
....

THE FRUIT OF THE SPIRIT IS
GENTLENESS

n recent years it has become popular to challenge or belittle the first verse of Charles Wesley's children's hymn:

> Gentle Jesus, meek and mild,
> Look upon a little child,
> Pity my simplicity,
> Suffer me to come to thee.
> *(The Song Book of The Salvation Army, 793)*

The objections have usually centred round the use of the word "gentle" in describing Jesus. Some people just don't like it.

It's true that Jesus was strong, determined, courageous and firm, but none of these qualities should detract from the fact that he was gentle — and that he said he was gentle.

When Jesus was inviting burdened disciples to come to him for rest, he used these words: "Take my yoke upon you and learn from me, for I am gentle and humble in heart, and you will find rest for your souls" (Matthew 11:29). It's natural that he would emphasise his gentleness and humility when encouraging people to trust him, but he was also inviting people to "learn" from him. If we are to learn from him, we are to be gentle too. It is a fruit of the Spirit. It isn't an optional extra.

The gentleness of Jesus was not only foretold by the prophet Zechariah (9:9), but also embraced by Jesus himself on Palm Sunday and recorded by Matthew (21:5): "See, your King comes to you, gentle and riding on a donkey".

Paul uses the gentleness of Jesus as an example of how the wayward and argumentative Corinthians should behave. In his second letter he writes, "by the meekness and gentleness of Christ, I appeal to you . . ." (10:1). That appeal remains today for all argumentative, strongly convinced Christians. Be gentle.

Being gentle is the opposite to using force. If God had wanted to use force to bring his wayward world under control he wouldn't have sent Jesus, his Son, as a baby. He would have chosen another option instead of crucifixion too. But he has rejected force. Force is meaningless in relationships and Christian faith is about relationship — especially with God.

In establishing the early Church, the new Christians made more than a few mistakes in this regard. The writers of the epistles were frequently calling their flocks to order, pleading for sensitive and gentle approaches. "Be completely humble and gentle" (Ephesians 4:2), writes Paul in Ephesians 4:2. That is complemented by "Let your gentleness be evident to all" in Philippians (4:5).

Giving advice on how to communicate with non-believers, Peter is keen to keep arrogance and any air of superiority out of things: "Always be prepared to give an answer to everyone who asks you to give the reason for the hope that you have. But do this with gentleness and respect . . ." (1 Peter 3:15).

God spoke to Elijah with a "gentle whisper" (1 Kings 19:12). He still does — to each of us. Crucial evidence of his Spirit working within us is our gentleness. ⊛

To consider

Why is gentleness often the forgotten quality of Jesus?

....
....
....
....
....
....
....
....
....

Are we awake to God's "gentle whisper"?

....
....
....
....
....
....
....

Why does Scripture emphasise the gentleness of Jesus?
(Zechariah 9:9; Matthew 11:29; 2 Corinthians 10:1)?

....
....
....
....
....
....
....
....
....

THE FRUIT OF THE SPIRIT IS
SELF-CONTROL

n his book *Renovation of the Heart*, Dallas Willard writes: "The strongest human will is the one that is surrendered to God's will and acts with it". This is self-control of the highest order. It is rooted in God and is empowered by God. It is a manifestation of the holy life — fruit of the Spirit's indwelling.

The human will and self-control do not go easily together. Surrendering our will for the greater good of those around us, demands effort. When strong desires take over, self-control is left floundering. Alexander Pope's collection of Moral Essays include this statement:

> "The ruling Passion, be it what it will,
> The ruling Passion conquers Reason still."

And so it does. Passion can be dangerous. Unchecked it can cause untold damage. Religious passion can be as damaging as any, as noted earlier. A reflection on the history of the Church and other religions gives more than enough proof. The crimes some people have committed passionately in "the name of God" are unspeakably perverse.

Addictions are another manifestation of not being in control. There are easily observed addictions — such as those involving substance abuse — but there are also less obvious addictions. These may include mindlessly watching the television, over-eating, collecting, arguing or working, for example. They all need facing up to and rectifying.

Proverbs 25:28 makes the comment that "Like a city whose walls are broken down is a man who lacks self-control". There is nothing commendable about it. Our defences have gone. Titus makes a number of references to the need to be self-controlled, but his injunction to be "self-controlled and pure" (2:5) gives a reminder that lack of self-control — giving into passions and desires — leads to impurity. It taints the holy life and alienates us from God.

At the heart of the problem is our free will. It has been given to us by God and he encourages us to use it wisely. He has chosen not to control us by force. His self-control as the Almighty God is beyond anything we can imagine. The surrender of Jesus to his Father's will — his prayer battle in Gethsemane and his surrender to the crucifixion — demonstrate a strength of willpower unsurpassed. It is this God who invites us to invite him to live his life in us, thus blending our wills. It is not achieved overnight!

Inviting the Holy Spirit into his life, Edwin Hatch wrote:

Breathe on me, breath of God,
Until my heart is pure,
Until with thee I will one will
To do and to endure.
(The Song Book of The Salvation Army, 189)

Dallas Willard added: "To succeed in identifying our will with God's will is not, as is often mistakenly thought, to have no will of our own . . . To have no will is impossible".

Our will deliberately chooses God's will for our lives — or not. The self-control we seek is not just for specific occasions. It is the self-control of a surrendered life — a life that willingly hands over control to Jesus. A holy life. ⚜

To consider

Why might lack of self-control lead to impurity? (Titus 2:5)

....
....
....
....
....

Try to examine the self-control of Jesus. (Matthew 26:41, 26:63 and 27:14)

....
....
....
....
....

How does self-control grow and develop within us?

....
....
....
....
....

In what way does the surrender of my will to God's will lead to holy living?

....
....
....
....
....
....

CALL TO HOLINESS

By the International Spiritual Life Commission*

We call salvationists worldwide to re-state and live out the doctrine of holiness in all its dimensions — personal, relational, social and political — in the context of our cultures and in the idioms of our day while allowing for, and indeed prizing, such diversity of experience and expression as is in accord with the Scriptures.

We affirm that God continues to desire and to command that his people be holy. For this Christ died, for this Christ rose again, for this the Spirit was given. We therefore determine to claim as God's gracious gift that holiness which is ours in Christ. We confess that at times we have failed to realise the practical consequences of the call to holiness within our relationships, within our communities and within our Movement. We resolve to make every effort to embrace holiness of life, knowing that this is only possible by means of the power of the Holy Spirit producing his fruit in us. ✺

*The International Spiritual Life Commission was formed by the General of The Salvation Army in the late 1990s to examine and emphasise those things which are and should be at the heart of the Army's spiritual life. There were 17 members (men and women, officers and soldiers, drawn from different countries and cultures). They met five times over a period of 18 months, each time for a week. They were assisted by corresponding members and correspondence from all parts of the Army world. Twelve calls to the Army were published by authority of the General in 1998. The call to holiness is the 10th of those calls. Robert Street was the Commission's chairman.

Notes